BLACK GEMS IN STEM

Copyright © 2018 Denise Smith-Archer

All rights reserved. No part of this publication may be reproduced in whole or in part, or stored in a retrieval system, or transmitted in any form or by any means, electronic, mechanical, photocopying, recording, scanning, or otherwise, without the prior written permission of the publisher.

ISBN: 978-0-692-06968-4

www.MiracleByDas.com

Printed in the USA

ACKNOWLEDGMENTS

As the African proverb goes: *"Mikono mingi kazi haba"* (Kiswahili) or "many hands make light work". Since the inception of the idea for this workbook, this proverb has shown itself over and over again, as family and friends continue to lend their hands. The names are many, but I wish to acknowledge here those who have played key roles.

First, I give thanks to my husband, who shares my passion for STEM education and community responsibility. Beyond backing me in everything I do, he played multiple roles in creating this workbook, serving as both contributing author and technical editor.

My mother, Patricia Smith, and my sister, Samora Smith make up my book production team. They have been and continue to be instrumental in the success of this workbook. Their support in editing, printing, publishing, and marketing has been crucial. My father, Dennis Smith, has been a huge supporter with regard to book promotion and distribution.

I would also like to extend thanks to various educators – Primrose and my cousin Mike among others – for their feedback and guidance.

To Osunkoya and Kelly, who are also educators in their own rights, as well as Samora, and the young people in you all's lives: thank you for your insight and assistance with the pilot study!

Thank you to everyone else who helped. It is my hope that the sense of community that went into making this workbook is felt by all of those who use it.

Asante sana!
(Thank you very much!)

TABLE OF CONTENTS

Introduction   1

Thomas Fuller   3

Benjamin Banneker   13

Lewis Latimer   25

George W. Carver   35

Madam C. J. Walker   45

Garrett A. Morgan   57

Marie Maynard Daly   67

Annie Easley   79

Patricia Bath   89

Mae C. Jemison   99

INTRODUCTION

I am an engineer – an engineer who strives to be both culturally and socially responsible. I am an engineer who truly believes that there is a need for more culturally and socially responsible professionals in science, technology, engineering, and math (STEM) to address many of the challenges that we face in our community and in our society. A major part of that responsibility is cultivating future leaders in STEM. One of the major hurdles in cultivating such leaders is that many of our children are neither being adequately prepared nor being encouraged to pursue careers in STEM fields.

The purpose of this workbook is to help address both of those issues by: (1) strengthening the students' core fundamentals of education (reading, writing, and arithmetic) and (2) featuring individuals in STEM who can serve as role models for our children. Each section of this workbook consists of: a biographical passage; reading comprehension questions; writing problems; mathematics problems; and two activities.

- *__Biographical Passages__* – The biographical passages are either short biographies or historical fiction stories about the featured individual. Emphasis, in these passages, is placed on the individual's contribution to the STEM fields.
- *__Reading Comprehension Questions__* – Following each passage is a set of multiple choice questions related to the reading. The question types that can be found in these sections are inference, vocabulary-in-context, main idea, detail, and tone.
- *__Writing Problems__* – The writing problems involve identifying and correcting grammatical errors. One section includes a short writing prompt in lieu of the problems.
- *__Mathematics Problems__* – The math section consists of multiple choice word problems. The math concepts that are covered in these problems involve arithmetic, algebra, and geometry.
- *__Activities__* – In addition to the educational aspect of the workbook, there are engaging activities at the end of each section. These activities include crossword puzzles, word searches, design activities, critical thinking exercises, and more. Even though all of these activities are not directly educational, they all have educational value. Furthermore, many of these activities integrate the arts into STEM (STEAM) by emphasizing the inherent role that art plays in STEM fields through activities such as designing and drawing. STEAM is also evident throughout the workbook by way of the illustrations that are used to complement the passages, questions, and activities.

The material in this workbook covers topics that fourth and fifth graders should be familiar with. On that note, the problems were developed with the various domains and clusters of the Common Core Standards used as reference points. Nevertheless, some of the problems are designed to be challenging to allow for continued academic growth.

In addition to strengthening reading, writing, and math skills, this workbook engages the students with questions similar in structure to those found on the SAT. This provides students with early exposure to the essence of the exam without diminishing the learning process by "teaching to the test".

As you will notice, the order of the featured Black Gems in STEM is, for the most part, the men followed by the women. This is by no means done in a patriarchal spirit. This is a result of ordering the featured individuals by birth year. While we could have chosen to organize the individuals another way, ordering them by birth year demonstrates the reality of the situation. This reality is that women entered into STEM fields, at least in a formal manner, much later than men. It is our job then, to prepare our girls, just as much as we prepare our boys, to actively pursue and succeed in STEM fields. I envision this workbook being used as a tool for such preparation, through academic development and the building of self-efficacy.

Parents, teachers, and students, I hope that you enjoy using this workbook as much as I enjoyed crafting it!

Denise Smith-Archer

THOMAS FULLER

THOMAS FULLER
"The Famous African Calculator"

I was born in 1710 in Africa – between two countries that are now known as Liberia and Benin. In 1724, I was kidnapped and then shipped to the United States of America and forced to work as a slave. I was the property of Presley Cox and Elizabeth Cox of Alexandria, Virginia.

Slaves were forbidden to learn in the USA, so I didn't know how to read or write. Nevertheless, I was a master with numbers. I had developed most of my math skills while I was in Africa. Traditional African mathematics education was the reason that I was so good at math. In the USA, I continued to teach myself how to do calculations quickly in my head. A little while after my owners had discovered this talent that I had, word got around that I was a math genius. There were two White gentlemen, in particular, who set out to find me to finally see for themselves what everyone else was telling them that I can do with numbers.

I ended up being used in the antislavery movement. There were a lot of White people who believed that Black people were inferior to them. They thought that Black people were not as good or smart as them. People used that idea of Black people being inferior to White people to help justify slavery. Abolitionists, individuals who fought to end slavery, ended up using me as an example to prove to people that Black people were extremely intelligent and had just as much mental capability as anyone else.

I am Thomas Fuller, the Famous African Calculator.

READING

The following questions are related to the passage about Thomas Fuller. For each question, select the best answer based on the information that you read in the passage.

1. The primary purpose of this passage is to
    a) teach the reader about countries in Africa.
    b) teach the reader about the history of the United States.
    c) tell the reader about the family that Thomas Fuller worked for.
    d) have a discussion about abolitionists.
    e) tell the reader a brief story of Thomas Fuller's life and math skills.

2. As used in line 7, the word "forbidden" means
    a) encouraged.
    b) irritated.
    c) happy.
    d) not allowed.
    e) reminded.

3. The author of this passage would most likely DISAGREE with which of the following statements about Thomas Fuller?
    a) He was smart.
    b) He was hardworking.
    c) He was very good at math.
    d) He was not helpful to the anti-slavery movement.
    e) He was born in Africa.

5

4. In line 13, the phrase "word got around" means that
   a) nobody believed Fuller's ability.
   b) Fuller's owners were talking bad about him.
   c) nobody cared.
   d) people were spreading the news.
   e) it was just a joke.

5. As used in line 20, the word "inferior" means
   a) sleepy.
   b) not as good as.
   c) scared.
   d) better than.
   e) funny.

WRITING

The following sentences test your ability to recognize grammatical errors. The sentences have either one error or no error at all. If the sentence has an error, circle the underlined part that contains the error. If the sentence does not contain an error, circle the choice that says "NO ERROR". After you make your selection, explain why you chose your answer.

Example: (many) people believe that slavery no longer <u>exists</u>, but the practice of slavery <u>continues</u> to this day. <u>NO ERROR</u>
Explanation: The error in this sentence is that "many" is not capitalized. The first word in a sentence should be capitalized. The error can be corrected by changing the lowercase "m" to an uppercase "M".

1. Thomas Fuller <u>were</u> born in Africa and <u>was forced</u> to go to the United States of America <u>as a teenager</u>. <u>NO ERROR</u>

    Explanation: _____
    _____
    _____

2. Black people <u>who were</u> enslaved <u>were not</u> allowed to read or write, because <u>their masters</u> did not want them to be smart. <u>NO ERROR</u>

    Explanation: _____
    _____
    _____

3. Liberia <u>and</u> Benin <u>is</u> countries <u>in</u> Africa. <u>NO ERROR</u>

   Explanation:_____

   _____

   _____

4. Traditional African mathematics <u>teached</u> me all that I <u>needed to know</u> to become a <u>master mathematician</u>. <u>NO ERROR</u>

   Explanation:_____

   _____

   _____

5. The purpose of <u>the</u> antislavery movement, as <u>its</u> name implies, <u>was to</u> end slavery. <u>NO ERROR</u>

   Explanation:_____

   _____

   _____

MATH

In this section, you are presented with math problems and a set of answer choices. Read each problem carefully. Then, solve each problem to choose the best answer.

1. In order to convert from minutes to seconds, you have to
    a) divide by 60.
    b) subtract 60.
    c) do nothing.
    d) add 60.
    e) multiply by 60.

2. Thomas Fuller was asked how many seconds there are in a year and a half. He answered the question in 2 minutes! Now you try it! How many seconds are there in 4 hours and 7 minutes?
    a) 42 seconds
    b) 247 seconds
    c) 420 seconds
    d) 14,400 seconds
    e) 14,820 seconds

3. Thomas Fuller was born in 1710. In 1724, he was kidnapped and shipped to the United States. How old was Thomas Fuller when he was kidnapped and shipped to the United States?
    a) 7 years old
    b) 14 years old
    c) 22 years old
    d) 24 years old
    e) 34 years old

4. Thomas was able to perform calculations like converting distances from miles to feet. How many feet are in 3 miles if 1 mile equals 5,280 feet?
    a) 1,760 feet
    b) 2,640 feet
    c) 5,280 feet
    d) 10,560 feet
    e) 15,840 feet

5. Traditional African mathematics is even seen in African architecture. For example, a village made up of circular houses may be arranged in a circle. If there are eight equally-spaced houses in a circular village, like the one shown below, what is the angle between each house?
    a) 15°
    b) 30°
    c) 45°
    d) 90°
    e) 180°

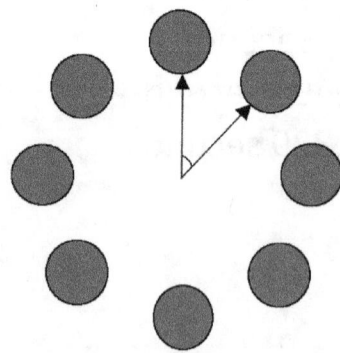

CROSSWORD PUZZLE

Fill in the cells with words in the word bank by using the clues given in the boxes. The clues have numbers next to them to indicate where to write in the word on the crossword puzzle (i.e., the answer to number 1 should be written across, starting in the cell labeled "1").

Across
1. the act of formally putting an end to a practice
3. the 3-letter abbreviation of the country where Thomas Fuller was forced to work as a slave
7. the continent that Thomas Fuller was born on
9. another word for smart
10. a math student or expert

Down
2. relating to ideas and behaviors that have been passed down usually within a culture
4. a special skill that allows a person to do something very well
5. the practice and economic system in which humans are classified as property
6. change from one form to another
8. the subject that deals with numbers and shapes

Word Bank
- mathematician
- abolition
- Africa
- mathematics
- USA
- talent
- intelligent
- slavery
- traditional
- convert

FRACTALS IN AFRICAN CULTURE

A fractal is a figure in which each part is the same shape as the larger figure. In many African cultures, fractals can be seen in village designs, hairstyles, spiritual rituals, and more. An example of a fractal is shown in Question 5 in the Math Section. Below are some more examples. After reviewing the fractals below, design one of your own.

Ethiopian Cross

Triangle made up of triangles

A fern leaf

BENJAMIN BANNEKER
"A Self-Educated Man"

"Dad, what time is it?" asked Kamau.

His dad turned around and pointed to the clock on the wall behind him. Kamau realized that it was 7:43 p.m., 17 minutes until bedtime. As he looked at the clock, he wondered how the clock knew the time. So he asked his dad, "How does the clock know the time?"

His dad smiled at him because he enjoyed his investigative nature. His dad, as usual, did not give him a direct answer; he started to tell Kamau a story about Benjamin Banneker.

"Benjamin Banneker was a self-taught mathematician, astronomer, inventor, writer, and compiler of almanacs," he began. "He was able to teach himself by reading books and studying different things."

"Dad, what does this have to do with the clock?" Kamau asked.

"Be patient young one," he replied. "Benjamin learned a lot by exploring things he saw around him. The first time Benjamin saw a timepiece was when his friend wore one. His friend used it to tell time. Benjamin, intrigued by the timepiece, asked his friend if he could borrow it. Benjamin took it apart to learn how it worked. After studying the timepiece, Benjamin built a watch out of wood. The watch that he built told the correct time for almost 40 years!"

30   Kamau started wondering if he could be like Benjamin Banneker and figure out what made clocks work. He asked his dad, "Can I take apart our clock to figure out how it works?"

    His dad replied, "Sure son, I will get my tools tomorrow and we can take it apart and investigate!"

35

    Kamau went to bed that night excited, wondering what was making the hands on the clock go around and around.

READING

The following questions are related to the passage about Benjamin Banneker. For each question, select the best answer based on the information that you read in the passage.

1. As used in line 9 of the passage, the word "investigative" means interested in
    a) being a police detective.
    b) making up a reason.
    c) making an educated guess.
    d) learning how something works.
    e) finding something.

2. The main character of this story is
    a) Kamau's dad.
    b) Benjamin Banneker.
    c) Kamau.
    d) the clock.
    e) Benjamin Banneker's friend.

3. In line 13 of the passage, the word "self-taught" means
    a) to learn by going to school.
    b) to be taught by your father.
    c) to teach other people.
    d) to learn by teaching yourself.
    e) to not learn at all.

4. As used in line 23, another name for a "timepiece" is
    a) the sun.
    b) an alarm clock.
    c) a watch.
    d) part-time.
    e) a type of student.

5. The main idea of this passage is that
    a) Benjamin Banneker loved making clocks, but his friend did not.
    b) boys named Kamau are smart.
    c) Kamau's dad told him a story about clocks.
    d) everyone needs to learn astronomy.
    e) Kamau was inspired to learn more about how clocks work after his dad told him a story about Benjamin Banneker.

WRITING

The following sentences test your ability to recognize grammatical errors. The sentences have either one error or no error at all. If the sentence has an error, circle the underlined part that contains the error. If the sentence does not contain an error, circle the choice that says "NO ERROR". After you make your selection, explain why you chose your answer.

Example: Using wood, Benjamin carved ⓐ enlarged <u>replica</u> of each part of <u>the watch</u>. <u>NO ERROR</u>
Explanation: The word "a" should be replaced by the word "an". The word "an" should be used before words that start with a vowel.

1. Benjamin Banneker was <u>also</u> a <u>surveyor, someone</u> who measures and records information about <u>areas of land</u> prior to construction.

    <u>NO ERROR</u>

    Explanation:_____
    _____
    _____

2. <u>From</u> 1792 to 1802, Banneker <u>publish</u> an annual <u>Farmers'</u> Almanac.

    <u>NO ERROR</u>

    Explanation:_____
    _____
    _____

3. Banneker <u>used his</u> reputation to <u>promote</u> the elimination <u>of</u> racism and war. <u>NO ERROR</u>

   Explanation:_____

   _____

   _____

4. In <u>1789, Benjamin</u> predicted a solar <u>eclipse that</u> same year, he <u>was</u> appointed to the <u>President's</u> Capital Commission. <u>NO ERROR</u>

   Explanation:_____

   _____

   _____

5. Benjamin's <u>almanacs</u> included anti-slavery <u>speeches</u> and <u>Essays</u> from England and America. <u>NO ERROR</u>

   Explanation:_____

   _____

   _____

MATH

In this section, you are presented with math problems and a set of answer choices. Read each problem carefully. Then, solve each problem to choose the best answer.

1. There is an average of 2.5 solar eclipses every year. About how many solar eclipses will occur in 4 years?
    a) 5 eclipses
    b) 7.5 eclipses
    c) 8 eclipses
    d) 10 eclipses
    e) 12 eclipses

2. In the reading passage, when Kamau looked at the clock, he saw that it was 7:43 p.m. and he only had 17 minutes until bedtime. What time was Kamau's bedtime?
    a) 7:26 p.m.
    b) 7:43 p.m.
    c) 8:00 p.m.
    d) 8:17 p.m.
    e) 8:43 p.m.

3. The minute hand on a clock moves once every minute. How many times does the minute hand move between 10:15 a.m. and 11:30 a.m.?
    a) 15 times
    b) 30 times
    c) 45 times
    d) 75 times
    e) 115 times

4. If the almanac says that sunrise is at 6 a.m. and sunset is at 8 p.m. tomorrow, how many hours of sunlight will there be tomorrow?
    a) 2 hours
    b) 6 hours
    c) 8 hours
    d) 12 hours
    e) 14 hours

5. Benjamin Banneker played a role in designing Washington, D.C., the nation's capital. The initial design of Washington, D.C. was a square, measuring 10 miles on each side. What was the perimeter of the initial design?
    a) 10 miles
    b) 20 miles
    c) 40 miles
    d) 100 miles
    e) 400 miles

WORD SEARCH PUZZLE

```
A G M H D C X E Y L A F W R S
S O L A R Q H U E H B R G W A
C S V U T G I P C L O C K X S
V P L Q C H Y Z Z M N L T J T
G X S U R V E Y I N G G C R R
E I O R A C N M N Y O Z E Y O
X N Y H D U G V A P E H R V N
L R T Q T L T A E T L O I N O
O E F A L M A N A C I L H H M
C Q R Y O U E R P S T C F V Y
K N D O D R C I E V Q O S P Q
Z A C W A E P A S T R O N O C
Q P S O K P O P N P E Q M V C
D P N O G R L T M Z R J E Y R
W X T A R C H I T E C T R M L
```

ALMANAC – a yearly publication with information about the weather, tides, sunrises, and sunsets
ARCHITECT – a person who designs buildings
ASTRONOMY – the study of stars, planets, and other celestial bodies
CLOCK – a device that tells time
MATHEMATICS – the study of numbers, shapes, and patterns
SURVEYING – using math to examine and record the features of land
SOLAR – related to the sun

DESIGN A COMMUNITY

Benjamin Banneker was a surveyor. He assisted in surveying the nation's capital, Washington, D.C. Surveying is a very important part of planning a community. Plan and create a community by drawing the things that the people living in the community need. Think about places such as where people can get food, learn, and work.

LEWIS LATIMER
"Electrical Engineer"

Today is February 19, 1881 and my hard work has finally paid off! I just patented my light bulb. You see, Thomas Edison developed a rather useful incandescent light (a light that glows from being heated). The light that Edison created consists of a wire filament inside of a glass bulb. When electricity is sent through the wire filament, which is usually made of bamboo, paper, or thread, the filament becomes so hot that it starts to glow. While the light that he created is a big contribution to the electric industry, it burns out too quickly.

While the electric companies were excited about Edison's invention, they still realized that to profit from the light, someone would first have to come up with a light that could burn for a longer period. There were plenty of people who were trying to make improvements to the light that Edison had invented. I was one of those people. I put a lot of time and effort into figuring out what could be done to make the light last longer. When I tell you that I worked hard, **that is exactly what I mean!**

Not only did I find a way to produce longer lasting light bulbs, but I also found a way to make the manufacturing of carbon filaments less expensive. My invention differed from the past light bulbs because I used different shapes of fibrous materials stuffed in pieces of cardboard. This prevents the carbon from breaking, allowing the bulb to burn longer.

For me, this achievement is only the beginning. I am looking forward to doing many more great things!

-Lewis Latimer

READING

The following questions are related to the passage about Lewis Latimer. For each question, select the best answer based on the information that you read in the passage.

1. The phrase in parentheses "(a light that glows from being heated)" in lines 3-4 is used to
    a) encourage the reader to use incandescent lights.
    b) explain the definition of an "incandescent light".
    c) give an example of what Edison did for fun.
    d) confuse the reader.
    e) explain how Edison's light worked.

2. The word "improvements" in line 14 could be replaced by all of the following EXCEPT
    a) advancements.
    b) upgrades.
    c) developments.
    d) money.
    e) enhancements.

3. All of the following can be inferred from the reading EXCEPT
    a) Latimer was a hard worker.
    b) Thomas Edison and Lewis Latimer did not like each other.
    c) Thomas Edison was also an inventor.
    d) Latimer was very smart.
    e) Latimer likely accomplished other achievements later in life.

4. The purpose of the bolded words in line 17 in the passage ("...**that is exactly what I mean**") is most likely to
    a) let the readers know that Lewis did not do any work.
    b) emphasize that Lewis Latimer worked very hard.
    c) suggest that Lewis Latimer was just doing this to get money.
    d) define what it means to work hard.
    e) discuss the steps to create a light bulb.

5. If the passage had a title, which title would most appropriately represent what the passage is about?
    a) All About Light Bulbs
    b) Guidelines to Using Electricity Safely
    c) The Day I Patented My Improved Light Bulb Invention
    d) A Conversation with Latimer and Edison
    e) The Life and Times of Lewis Latimer

WRITING

The passage below is an example of a persuasive paragraph about Lewis Latimer. While you read the passage, take note of strategies that the author uses to build the argument.

Lewis Latimer is one of the most influential inventors in history. He is responsible for many helpful inventions. For example, Lewis Latimer developed an improved version of the light bulb that Thomas Edison created. Latimer's improved version allowed the light bulb to work longer and to be produced at a much cheaper cost. In addition to the light bulb, Lewis developed an improved toilet system for trains, a safety elevator, electrical fireworks, locking racks, a book supporter to help keep books organized on shelves, and a device that keeps rooms cooler and gets rid of bad odors and germs. He also wrote a book on electric lighting and how it works. He even worked as an electrical expert for Thomas Edison. When he was not working on his own inventions, he was often helping other people get licenses for their inventions. Despite his many inventions and contributions to society, other people were often given credit for his work. Nevertheless, he still worked hard and overcame racism and discrimination, while being a wonderful husband and father, to become one of the greatest inventors of all time.

Using the lines below, write an essay explaining what the author's main argument is. Additionally, identify some of the key points the author made to support that argument. Explain how those key points helped to strengthen the argument. **DO NOT explain whether or not you agree with the author's argument.**

_____
_____
_____
_____
_____

MATH

In this section, you are presented with math problems and a set of answer choices. Read each problem carefully. Then, solve each problem to choose the best answer.

1. Lewis Latimer's parents were born into slavery. They escaped from slavery in Norfolk, Virginia to freedom in Boston, Massachusetts in 1842. If Lewis Latimer was born six years after his parents escaped from slavery, what year was he born?
    a) 1842
    b) 1846
    c) 1848
    d) 1850
    e) 1852

2. Light bulb A lasted 9 hours. Light bulb B lasted three times as long as light bulb A. How long did light bulb B last?
    a) 9 hours
    b) 12 hours
    c) 18 hours
    d) 27 hours
    e) 45 hours

3. Electric power is often measured in kilowatts (kW). Energy, which is the amount of power over a period of time, is commonly measured in kilowatt hours (kWh). So, the amount of energy consumed (used) by a light bulb can be calculated by multiplying the power of the light bulb by the amount of time the light bulb is used. If you turn on a 2-kW light bulb for 8 hours, how much energy is consumed?
    a) 2 kWh
    b) 6 kWh
    c) 8 kWh
    d) 14 kWh
    e) 16 kWh

4. Lewis Latimer worked for Crosby and Gould, a patent law firm which prepared and reviewed applications for inventions, for 11 years. He started working as an office boy making $3 per week. He became the chief draftsman in which he was making $20 per week. How much more did he make per week as a draftsman than as an office boy?
    a) $3
    b) $17
    c) $20
    d) $23
    e) $60

5. As mentioned in Question 4, Latimer made $20 per week as a draftsman. Because of racial discrimination, however, the other draftsmen made $5 more than Latimer. Which equation could be used to calculate how much the other draftsmen made per week?
    a) 20 ÷ 5
    b) 20 - 5
    c) 20 + 5
    d) 20 x 5
    e) 20^5

DEFINE AND FIND!

light bulb _____
filament _____
incandescent _____
glass _____
electrical _____
wire _____
carbon _____
circuit _____
invention _____
patent _____

c	a	p	a	t	e	n	t	a	t	r	b	c	l	y
b	a	n	q	y	a	d	u	t	r	l	f	a	r	i
i	g	r	p	o	j	b	q	n	x	o	c	f	v	g
e	w	t	b	y	u	c	s	e	o	i	l	p	l	z
a	d	s	t	o	h	m	d	v	r	b	i	d	v	g
t	f	l	g	k	n	e	h	t	y	j	g	z	m	l
f	b	s	b	q	a	v	c	b	n	c	h	m	x	a
i	n	c	a	n	d	e	s	c	e	n	t	w	e	s
l	t	w	i	o	l	o	q	r	n	u	b	h	o	s
a	h	i	m	e	p	z	p	r	j	e	u	s	c	y
m	f	k	s	k	d	x	k	u	v	q	l	e	l	g
e	p	x	j	s	w	i	r	e	l	r	b	t	f	q
n	s	o	m	p	d	n	w	q	j	w	k	c	t	h
t	j	i	n	v	e	n	t	i	o	n	y	u	z	z
o	l	g	e	c	i	r	c	u	i	t	i	u	a	u

IT'S ELECTRIC!

Light bulbs are not the only items that use electricity. Many of us are fortunate to have daily access to electricity. Circle the items that require electricity to work. Feel free to color the items as well!

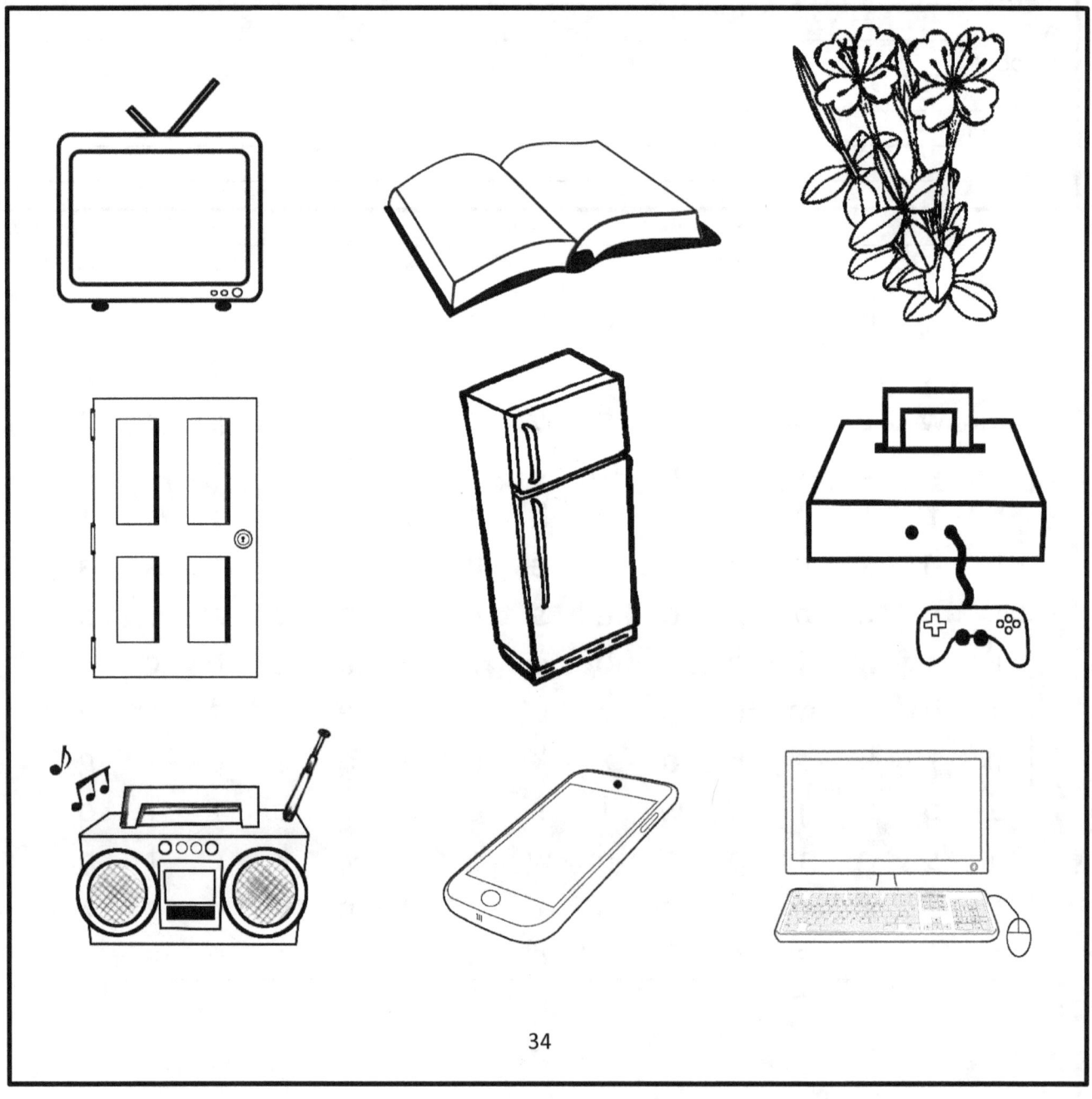

GEORGE WASHINGTON CARVER
"The Plant Doctor"

George Washington Carver was born in Missouri in 1864, one year before slavery was abolished by the passing of the 13th Amendment to the United States Constitution. Growing up, George loved learning about plants and animals. He also really enjoyed art. After graduating from high school in Kansas, he took art classes at Simpson College, and then transferred to Iowa State College. At Iowa State, George earned a bachelor's degree and a master's degree in science; he studied plants to become a botanist.

After graduating from Iowa State, George became the first Black professor at the college. While teaching at Iowa State College, George was contacted by Booker T. Washington, who had started an all-Black college in Tuskegee, Alabama, called the Tuskegee Institute. Booker T. Washington asked George to lead the agriculture department at the college. George accepted the position and started teaching at Tuskegee Institute in 1896. George taught there for the rest of his life.

While at Tuskegee Institute, George conducted a lot of research and did plenty of experiments to help farmers. He helped farmers by teaching them how to rotate their crops in order to make the soil better. He also helped farmers by teaching them new ways to use the crops that they grew. George is most famous for discovering over 300 uses for peanuts! Some food products from peanuts that George discovered were peanut butter, peanut tutti frutti bars, cooking oil, and peanut meal (used to feed animals). There were also many non-food items that George discovered could be made from peanuts, such as lotion, shampoo, and paint.

READING

The following questions are related to the passage about George Washington Carver. For each question, select the best answer based on the information that you read in the passage.

1. In what year was slavery abolished by the passing of the 13th Amendment to the United States Constitution?
    a) 1776
    b) 1863
    c) 1864
    d) 1865
    e) 1943

2. As used in line 9, what is the meaning of the word "botanist"?
    a) a type of plant
    b) a president
    c) a scientist that studies plants
    d) something that George loved to do
    e) a teacher

3. Who was the founder of the all-Black college, Tuskegee Institute, in Tuskegee, Alabama?
    a) George Washington Carver
    b) Martin Luther King Jr.
    c) Frederick Douglass
    d) Booker T. Washington
    e) George Washington

4. Reading lines 10-11, the reader can infer that a professor is
    a) a person who works as a landscaper at a college.
    b) any person who teaches.
    c) someone who studies plants.
    d) a person who teaches at a college.
    e) a type of student.

5. The main purpose of this passage is to
    a) teach about the different uses of peanuts.
    b) teach about Tuskegee Institute.
    c) show that George Washington Carver loved art.
    d) inform the reader about George's life and accomplishments.
    e) talk about Iowa State College.

WRITING

The following sentences test your ability to recognize grammatical errors. The sentences have either one error or no error at all. If the sentence has an error, circle the underlined part that contains the error. If the sentence does not contain an error, circle the choice that says "NO ERROR". After you make your selection, explain why you chose your answer.

Example: George Washington <u>Carver's</u> nickname (were) the "Wizard <u>of</u> Tuskegee". <u>NO ERROR</u>

Explanation: The sentence only mentions one (singular) nickname. Therefore, the verb should be singular. So, "were" should be changed to "was".

1. George <u>growed</u> up as a young boy <u>in</u> Missouri until he <u>went</u> to school.

    <u>NO ERROR</u>

    Explanation: _____

    _____

    _____

2. Since George <u>liked</u> plants <u>and</u> science, he <u>decided</u> to study botany.

    <u>NO ERROR</u>

    Explanation: _____

    _____

    _____

3. <u>Many</u> farmers made more money from <u>there</u> crops after George Washington Carver showed them different ways to use <u>them</u>. <u>NO ERROR</u>

   Explanation:_____

   _____

   _____

4. George also loved <u>art, so</u> he took art <u>classes</u> at Simpson College <u>after</u> high school. <u>NO ERROR</u>

   Explanation:_____

   _____

   _____

5. During the <u>time</u> of George W. Carver's <u>life people</u> in the South <u>called</u> peanuts "goobers". <u>NO ERROR</u>

   Explanation:_____

   _____

   _____

MATH

In this section, you are presented with math problems and a set of answer choices. Read each problem carefully. Then, solve each problem to choose the best answer.

1. A peanut plant grows, on average, 5 centimeters (cm) per month. If a farmer plants the peanut plant seeds on March 1st, how tall will the plants be when he is ready to harvest (pick) the plants on August 1st?
    a) 10 cm
    b) 15 cm
    c) 20 cm
    d) 25 cm
    e) 30 cm

2. A farmer has a plot of land that has 5 rows. If she plants 20 peanut seeds per row, how many total peanut seeds does she have in the plot of land?
    a) 20
    b) 50
    c) 100
    d) 140
    e) 200

3. Each peanut plant produces between 25 and 50 peanuts and the farmer wants to put the peanuts from 4 plants into bags. If each bag can hold 10 peanuts, what is the most number of bags the farmer will need?
   a) 8
   b) 10
   c) 14
   d) 18
   e) 20

4. George Washington Carver started teaching at Tuskegee Institute in the year 1896, and taught there until he died in 1943. How many years did George teach at Tuskegee Institute?
   a) 26 years
   b) 30 years
   c) 43 years
   d) 47 years
   e) 53 years

5. George Washington Carver discovered 12 ways to make beverages out of peanuts. If he discovered 5 times as many food items from peanuts than beverages, how many food items did he discover from peanuts?
   a) 7
   b) 17
   c) 25
   d) 50
   e) 60

WORD SEARCH PUZZLE

```
A G R H D T S E Y J H F D R Y
D G R D E A H U F H F R G W S
C S R U I G I P E A N U T X K
V P L Q C R Y Z Z M N L T J J
G A T S C I E N T I S T C R Q
F I O S A C N J N Y O Z E Y N
C N Y H D U G V R P E H R V D
S T M Q T L T A E E L O I N H
P E F B O T A N Y N S L H H P
W R R Y O U E R P S T X F V S
T N D O D R C I E V Q O A P Q
P A C Q A E P F R L I P R D C
V P S O K P O P N P E Q M V C
Q P N O G R L T M Z R J E Y R
F C I D P N I F T F U I R E F
```

AGRICULTURE – the scientific study of farming
BOTANY – the study of plants
FARMER – a person who grows food
INVENTOR – a person who creates something new
PAINTER – a person who creates visual art using paint
PEANUT – an oval seed of a plant that is eaten as a snack
PROFESSOR – a teacher at a college or university
SCIENTIST – a person who studies or is an expert in any of the sciences

TIME TO INVENT!

Get creative! Use the space below to draw any ideas you have for inventions made from peanuts!

I am not merely satisfied in making money for myself, for I am endeavoring to provide employment for hundreds of women of my race...I want to say to every [Black] woman present, don't sit down and wait for the opportunities to come. Get up and make them!

-Madam C. J. Walker

Madam C. J. Walker

"An Interview with the First Female Self-Made Millionaire in America"

Interviewer: Madam C. J. Walker, thank you so much for taking the time to sit down and talk with me. How are you doing?

Madam C. J. Walker: I am doing well. Thank you for asking.

Interviewer: So, I wanted to talk to you today about the story of your life —how you went from being the daughter of sharecroppers to being the first self-made woman millionaire in America. What inspired you to start your business?

Madam C. J. Walker: Well, I developed a scalp ailment that caused me to lose most of my hair. I experimented with different homemade remedies as well as products from the store. I eventually developed a remedy that helped me grow my hair back. That's how "Madam Walker's Wonderful Hair Grower", the popular scalp conditioning and healing formula, came to fruition.

Interviewer: Amazing! Did you sell your products by yourself?

Madam C. J. Walker: Oh no way! I started off with humble beginnings. My husband was very instrumental in the success of the company. By 1917, my company employed over 20,000 women who went door to door selling my products. Had it not been for the support of the community, both selling and buying the products, I would not have seen the success that I am seeing now.

Interviewer: With regard to the community supporting you, I've heard that you have given just as much support back to the community.

30 **Madam C. J. Walker:** Sure, you can say that. Once I moved to Harlem, New York with my daughter, I really became involved in politics. I feel that I have a responsibility to fight for justice and against inequality. So, I use my business and my resources to do just that.

READING

The following questions are related to the passage about Madam C. J. Walker. For each question, select the best answer based on the information that you read in the passage.

1. The main purpose of the first part of the discussion (lines 1—9) is to
    a) provide background on the interviewer.
    b) thank Madam C. J. Walker for coming.
    c) explain what a sharecropper is.
    d) set the tone for rest of the interview.
    e) determine when Madam C. J. Walker was born.

2. Based on the interview, Madam C. J. Walker was all of the following EXCEPT
    a) a mother.
    b) an entrepreneur.
    c) a medical doctor.
    d) a self-made millionaire.
    e) an inventor.

3. In line 11, the word "ailment" could be replaced by all of the words EXCEPT for
    a) condition.
    b) treatment.
    c) disorder.
    d) disease.
    e) illness.

4. The sentence "I experimented with..." (lines 12-13) suggests that Madam C. J. Walker
   a) looked up ingredients in a book.
   b) threw away all of her hair products.
   c) gave up on developing a product.
   d) stole a product and claimed it as her own.
   e) tested new ideas.

5. It can be inferred from the sentence "So, I use my business and my resources..." (lines 33-34) that Madam C. J. Walker
   a) was mean.
   b) kept all her money to herself.
   c) was not aware of inequalities around her.
   d) used her money to help others.
   e) threw her money away.

WRITING

The following sentences test your ability to recognize grammatical errors. The sentences have either one error or no error at all. If the sentence has an error, circle the underlined part that contains the error. If the sentence does not contain an error, circle the choice that says "NO ERROR". After you make your selection, explain why you chose your answer.

Example: Many <u>people</u> do not <u>know. that</u> Madam C. J. Walker's birth name <u>was</u> Sarah Breedlove. <u>NO ERROR</u>

Explanation: Including a period after "know" and before "that" creates sentence fragments. The sentence can be corrected by deleting the period.

1. The Madam C. J. Walker Manufacturing Company's headquarters <u>was</u> initially <u>in Denver</u> and <u>later</u> moved to Indianapolis. <u>NO ERROR</u>

    Explanation: _____
    _____
    _____

2. Madam C. J. <u>Walker's story</u> continues to be <u>a inspiration</u> to <u>many</u> entrepreneurs. <u>NO ERROR</u>

    Explanation: _____
    _____
    _____

3. Madam C. J. Walker <u>donated</u> money to scholarships for many <u>woman</u> at Tuskegee Institute, the NAACP, the YMCA, <u>and</u> other organizations and charities. <u>NO ERROR</u>

   Explanation: _____

   _____

   _____

4. The company also <u>had</u> a branch in Pittsburgh, <u>Which</u> was managed by Madam C. J. Walker's <u>daughter,</u> A'Lelia. <u>NO ERROR</u>

   Explanation: _____

   _____

   _____

5. Most of the <u>women</u> Madam C. J. Walker <u>employed</u> worked as saleswomen, going door to door <u>to</u> promote her hair- and skin-care products. <u>NO ERROR</u>

   Explanation: _____

   _____

   _____

MATH

In this section, you are presented with math problems and a set of answer choices. Read each problem carefully. Then, solve each problem to choose the best answer.

1. Madam C. J. Walker had to walk to and from school every day. If the school was 2 miles away from her house, how many miles did she have to walk each day?
    a) 1 mile
    b) 2 miles
    c) 4 miles
    d) 6 miles
    e) 20 miles

2. Madam Walker's Wonderful Hair Grower cost $0.50 per can. How many cans would a saleswoman need to sell to make $1,000?
    a) 50
    b) 100
    c) 1,000
    d) 1,500
    e) 2,000

3. Madam C. J. Walker was born in 1867. If she was about 38 years old when she started her company, around what year did she start her company?
    a) 1867
    b) 1905
    c) 1915
    d) 1938
    e) 1967

4. The exact number of salespeople that Madam C. J. Walker employed is not known. If we assume she had 20,000 salespeople working in 10 states, what is the average number of salespeople in each of those 10 states?
    a) 10
    b) 20
    c) 200
    d) 2,000
    e) 20,000

5. When Madam C. J. Walker worked as a laundress, she made about $1.50 per day. If she worked five days per week, about how much did she make in a week?
    a) $1.50
    b) $5.50
    c) $7.50
    d) $15.00
    e) $17.50

ENTREPRENEURSHIP

Entrepreneurship is the activity of starting a business. So, an entrepreneur is a person who starts a business. Differing from other business owners, entrepreneurs typically take on great financial risks. This means that there is a chance that their business will not do so well. However, there is also a chance that their business will do very well, like Madam C. J. Walker's business!

Have you ever thought of being a business owner? Give entrepreneurship a try. Fill out the plan below to get started on your own business.

Business Name
◊ What will the name of your company be?

Products or Services
◊ What products will you sell or what services will you provide?
    ⇒
    ⇒

Getting Started
◊ What steps do you need to take to get started?
    ⇒
    ⇒

◊ What resources do you need to get started?
    ⇒
    ⇒

DESIGNING A LOGO

Now that you have come up with the idea for your business, design a logo. A logo is an image that identifies a company or product. Get started by looking at logos from other companies. You can look at logos on stores, food packaging, clothes, and other common items.

GARRETT A. MORGAN
"Entrepreneur & Inventor"

I was born in Kentucky in 1877. I was the seventh of 11 children. I only had a fifth-grade education, but I moved to Ohio to learn more and to look for some job opportunities. I picked up a job at a sewing machine factory. I learned everything that I possibly could about the machines and how to fix them. I eventually developed an improved sewing machine and opened my own sewing machine repair business. I also made clothes and, later on, hair products. I invented many things.

There were two inventions, in particular, that most people would consider to be my most important contributions to society. One was a breathing device, also known to many people as the safety hood or the gas mask. This device provides a way for people who are exposed to smoke, toxic gases, and airborne pollutants – like soldiers and miners – to breathe better. The other invention was the traffic signal. Living in Cleveland, Ohio when automobiles first became popular, I experienced chaotic and unsafe traveling conditions. I was inspired to do something about this after witnessing a terrible crash between an automobile and a horse-drawn buggy. The version of the traffic signal that I invented controlled cars by telling drivers when to stop, when to go, and when to get ready to stop. A more modern version of the traffic signal is still used today to control traffic and help keep people safe.

I dedicated my life to coming up with creative ways to solve problems. In my mind, there wasn't a problem that I couldn't solve. I had confidence in myself and a desire to make other people's lives better.

READING

The following questions are related to the passage about Garrett A. Morgan. For each question, select the best answer based on the information that you read in the passage.

1. In the passage, all of the following are mentioned as inventions of Garrett A. Morgan, EXCEPT
    a) hair products.
    b) peanut butter.
    c) the traffic signal.
    d) the gas mask.
    e) an improved sewing machine.

2. In line 16, the word "chaotic" could be replaced with
    a) calm.
    b) smart.
    c) disorderly.
    d) fast.
    e) clean.

3. This passage would most likely be seen in
    a) an autobiography.
    b) a newspaper article.
    c) a dictionary.
    d) a text message.
    e) a comic strip.

4. The most appropriate title for this passage would be
    a) "How to Make a Sewing Machine".
    b) "Why People Can Breathe Better Now".
    c) "The Many Inventions of Garrett A. Morgan".
    d) "Clothes for Sale".
    e) "My Experience of Working in a Factory".

5. What can you infer about Garrett A. Morgan from reading the passage?
    a) He was bad when he was young.
    b) He only invented things to get rich.
    c) He enjoyed learning and inventing things to solve problems.
    d) He did not get along with his brothers and sisters.
    e) He played a lot of games.

WRITING

The following sentences test your ability to recognize grammatical errors. The sentences have either one error or no error at all. If the sentence has an error, circle the underlined part that contains the error. If the sentence does not contain an error, circle the choice that says "NO ERROR". After you make your selection, explain why you chose your answer.

Example: Garrett Morgan <u>used</u> his creativity and <u>concern for people</u> to (solved) problems. <u>NO ERROR</u>
Explanation: The correct verb tense is solve. The phrase, "to solve", is an infinitive verb phrase ("to" + verb). The verb in an infinitive phrase should be in present tense.

1. Inventions <u>is</u> inspired <u>by</u> creativity <u>and imagination</u>. <u>NO ERROR</u>

    Explanation: _____
    _____
    _____

2. <u>On a traffic signal</u>, the red light <u>means "stop"</u> and the green light <u>means "go"</u>. <u>NO ERROR</u>

    Explanation: _____
    _____
    _____

3. When I <u>grow up</u>, I want <u>to be</u> an inventor <u>who invents things</u>.
   <u>NO ERROR</u>

   Explanation:_____

   _____

   _____

4. <u>In addition to</u> his other <u>endeavors,</u> Garrett Morgan started <u>a</u> newspaper for African-Americans. <u>NO ERROR</u>

   Explanation:_____

   _____

   _____

5. <u>Due to</u> racial discrimination in the <u>South, Morgan</u> had a hard time <u>sell</u> his gas masks to the fire departments. <u>NO ERROR</u>

   Explanation:_____

   _____

   _____

MATH

In this section, you are presented with math problems and a set of answer choices. Read each problem carefully. Then, solve each problem to choose the best answer.

1. The cycle length of a traffic signal can be defined as the time it takes for all phases of traffic to get a chance to go. One way to calculate the cycle length for a simple traffic signal is to add the lengths of time of the green, yellow, and red lights (green + yellow + red) for one direction of traffic. The cycle length of a particular traffic signal is 90 seconds. If, for a given direction, the yellow light is 5 seconds and the red light is 35 seconds, how long is the green light?
    a) 10 seconds
    b) 50 seconds
    c) 65 seconds
    d) 70 seconds
    e) 115 seconds

2. Garrett A. Morgan was born in 1877. If he invented the safety hood in 1914, about how old was he when he invented the safety hood?
    a) 14 years old
    b) 24 years old
    c) 30 years old
    d) 37 years old
    e) 77 years old

3. Let's assume that Garrett A. Morgan made a total of $5200 by selling 100 gas masks. If he sold all of the gas masks for the same price, what was the price of each mask?
    a) $35
    b) $52
    c) $55
    d) $100
    e) $520

4. When Garrett A. Morgan invented his new and improved version of the traffic signal in 1923, there were 15 million registered cars in the United States. Which of the following values is NOT equal to 15 million?
    a) 1.50×10^7
    b) 15×10^6
    c) 150×10^5
    d) 15000×10^2
    e) 1500×10^4

5. The safety hood had a long cylindrical tube that connected from the mask to the floor in order to filter out smoke. The shape of the tube was similar to the one shown in the figure below. If the radius, r, of the tube was 3 inches and the height, h, was 60 inches, what was the volume, V, of the tube?
    a) 60π inches^3
    b) 100π inches^3
    c) 180π inches^3
    d) 360π inches^3
    e) 540π inches^3

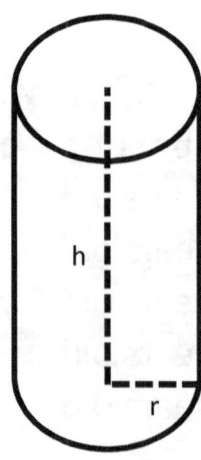

$$V = \pi \times r \times r \times h$$

THE GAS MASK

Innovation often means improving something that already exists. Garrett A. Morgan demonstrated innovation by creating an improved version of the gas mask. Using your creativity, develop your own version of a gas mask by adding to the template below.

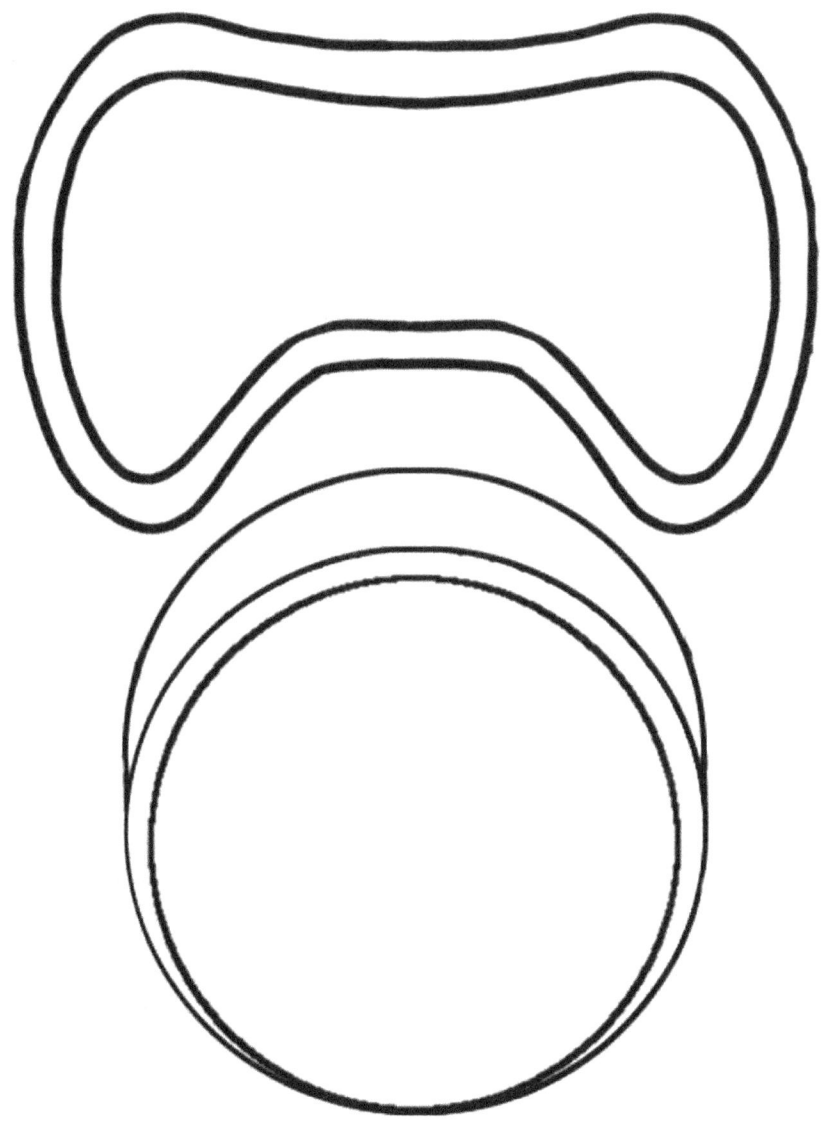

TRAFFIC CONTROL DEVICES

Traffic control devices include signals, signs, and markings. These devices are used to guide and control traffic. Common traffic control devices are shown below. Identify each one and write their meaning on the lines below.

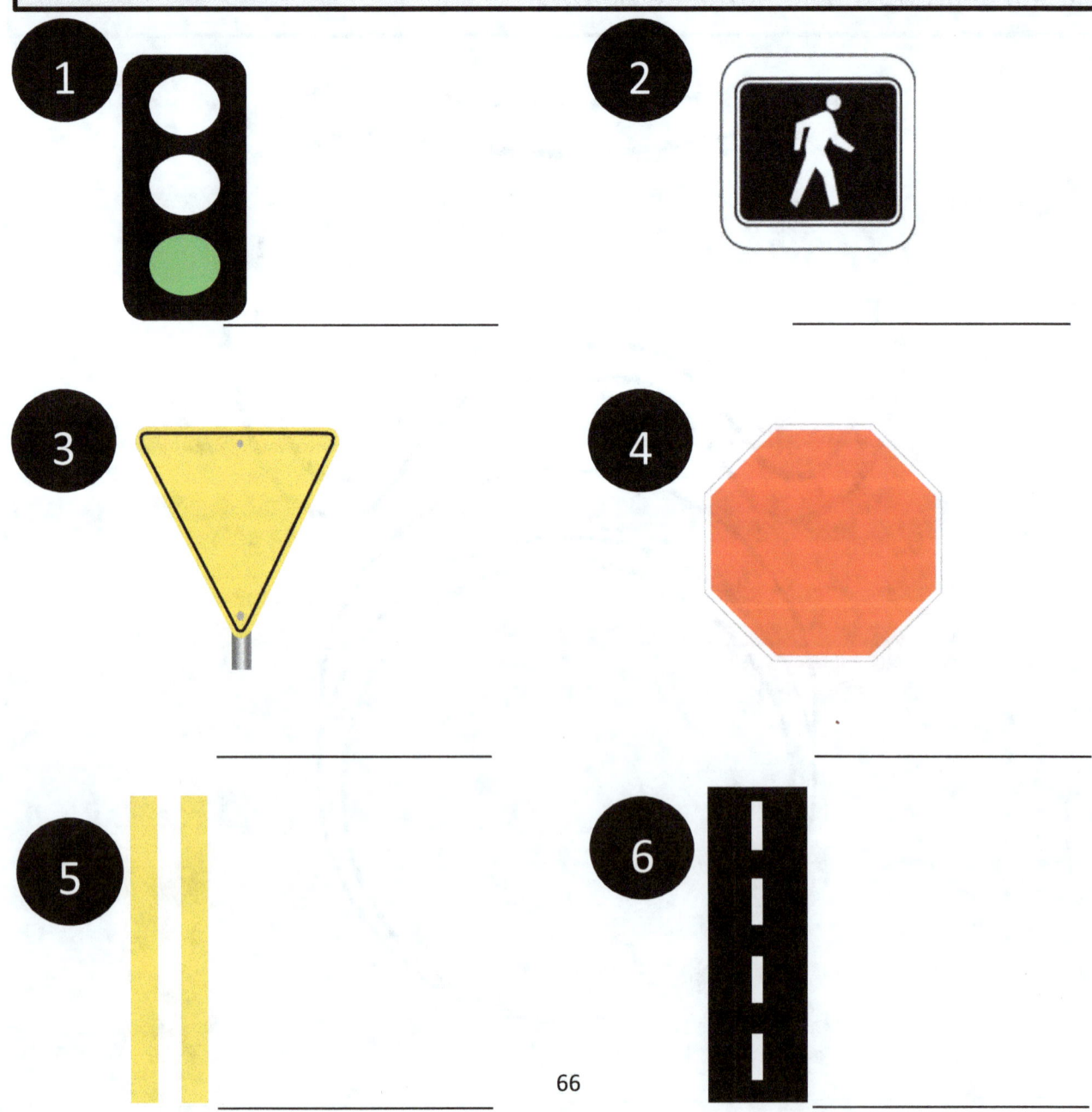

MARIE MAYNARD DALY

MARIE MAYNARD DALY
"A Pioneer in the Field of Chemistry"

The students were entering the classroom as the morning bell rang. They were both nervous and excited about their group presentations on influential people of color in science.

Mrs. Gray closed the classroom door. You could hear groups getting in their last-minute practice and checking their poster boards, props, and elaborate costumes. It wasn't too long before Mrs. Gray called the class to order. "Good morning, class! I hope you all are ready for your presentations today. We have a tight schedule and a lot of presentations to get through, so let's jump right in. Group 1, you're up!"

Group 1, composed of Tanya, Tishawn, and Briana, walked to the front of the classroom. They set their props up. Their poster board was titled "George Washington Carver: Botanist and Inventor". They spent the next 10 minutes talking about Mr. Carver's many inventions.

Group after group came to the front of the classroom and gave their presentations. Most of them were like the presentation done by Group 1 – informative, but not very interesting and engaging.

Jabari, Kenya, and Treyvon's group, Group 7, was up next. Something was different about this group. Unlike the groups that presented before them, this group had no props and no costumes. But Treyvon was carrying his phone and mini-speakers.

As the three group members walked to the front of the classroom, there was complete silence followed by a sudden outbreak of loud whispers. "Where are their props and costumes?" "Did they forget that we had presentations today?" "This is going to be interesting."

	Mrs. Gray, curious herself, looked at the group with a sense of confusion and then proceeded to ask the group if they had everything they needed for the presentation. Jabari confidently spoke up and replied "Yep, we sure do, Mrs. Gray!"

	"Okay, then - the floor is yours," Mrs. Gray replied.

	Jabari started the presentation off talking about the history of Hip-Hop. Certainly, everyone in the audience was confused. What could Hip-Hop possibly have to do with an influential person of color in science? Despite the teacher's confusion, she let him continue. Jabari concluded his introduction by saying: "And Hip-Hop has been used as a medium to tell stories. So, we present to you the story of Marie Maynard Daly." Treyvon cued the music on his phone and the group performed their song.

Jabari:
	Marie Maynard Daly was born in Queens
	Destined to be great – an intelligent, Black queen
	At a young age, she was taught to value education
	Always in pursuit of relevant information

	She studied chemistry in college, earned multiple degrees
	First Black woman in chemistry with a PhD
	After that she taught and conducted research
	Discovering new things was her passion and her work

Kenya:
	She explained the human body in more detail
	How proteins are made and help repair the cells
	How chemicals help with food digestion
	Her research provided answers to many questions

	Like what causes people to have heart attacks

        Like what causes people to have heart attacks
60   Looking for the answers, exploring the facts
        How are clogged arteries and high cholesterol related
        How does diet affect heart health and blood circulation

        Treyvon:
65   She was a big supporter of Black students in science
        At the medical and graduate schools they desired
        She started a scholarship to help them pay for school
        Go forward but give back, that's a good rule

70   And that is the life of Daly in a rap
        Committed to science and the community of Blacks
        We hope you enjoyed the rhymes we shared
        Using Hip-Hop for storytelling, to make you aware

75   Once they finished their rap, the class roared with applause. For the final 10 minutes of their presentation, they read the lyrics line by line. They explained what each line meant, elaborating on the different topics of Daly's life. Again, the class roared with applause.

80   "Excellent job!" Mrs. Gray exclaimed. "This group not only taught us about Marie Maynard Daly and Hip-Hop, but they taught us a valuable lesson as well. And that lesson is we should never limit ourselves by following the norm. This group was creative and showed us how to use a song to teach."

READING

The following questions are related to the passage about Marie Maynard Daly. For each question, select the best answer based on the information that you read in the passage.

1. The primary purpose of the first paragraph is to
    a) explain what "science" is.
    b) inform the reader of the topic of the passage.
    c) introduce the teacher.
    d) use the word "influential" in a sentence.
    e) explain that students must be in class before the bell rings.

2. The sentence starting on line 21, "Unlike the groups that had presented before them, this group had no props and no costumes", suggests that
    a) someone stole Group 7's props.
    b) you cannot give a presentation without props and costumes.
    c) Group 7 used props and costumes in past presentations.
    d) all the other groups had props and costumes.
    e) Group 7 told the teacher that they would have costumes.

3. The word "concluded", as used in line 38, means
    a) started.
    b) laughed.
    c) finished.
    d) forgot.
    e) dropped.

4. Which of the following words could be used to replace the word "medium" on line 39 without changing the meaning of the sentence?
    a) essay
    b) way
    c) middle
    d) high
    e) low

5. The teacher's statement "...we should never limit ourselves by following the norm" (lines 82-83) is primarily meant to convey the idea that
    a) it is okay to be different.
    b) being different is not a good idea.
    c) Group 7 did not do a good job.
    d) being creative will not get you a good grade.
    e) Hip-Hop should not be used to teach a lesson.

WRITING

The following sentences test your ability to recognize grammatical errors. The sentences have either one error or no error at all. If the sentence has an error, circle the underlined part that contains the error. If the sentence does not contain an error, circle the choice that says "NO ERROR". After you make your selection, explain why you chose your answer.

Example: A biochemist (are) someone who studies chemical processes that happen within living organisms. NO ERROR

Explanation: The word "are" should be replaced with "is" since "A biochemist" is a singular noun. The word "are" would be used if the plural form, "Biochemists", was used.

1. When Daly visited her grandparents, she would read her grandfathers books about scientists and their achievements. NO ERROR

    Explanation:_____
    _____
    _____

2. She received a award from the American Cancer Society to support her research and work. NO ERROR

    Explanation:_____
    _____
    _____

3. Daly was also inspired to study science because of her father, who started school to become a chemist, but did not have enough money to finish. NO ERROR

   Explanation:_____

   _____

   _____

4. Daly also studied the effects that cigarette smoke have on the lungs. NO ERROR

   Explanation:_____

   _____

   _____

5. The essay that Marie wrote for her PhD, also known as a thesis, is titled "A Study of the Products Formed by the Action of Pancreatic Amylase on Corn Starch". NO ERROR

   Explanation:_____

   _____

   _____

MATH

In this section, you are presented with math problems and a set of answer choices. Read each problem carefully. Then, solve each problem to choose the best answer.

1. Marie Maynard Daly was born in 1921 and received her PhD in 1947. At about what age did she receive her PhD?
    a) 16 years old
    b) 21 years old
    c) 26 years old
    d) 36 years old
    e) 47 years old

2. Cholesterol is a type of fat in your blood that helps your organs work. High cholesterol can lead to clogged arteries, which can increase your risk of heart attack and stroke. During his health screening, Deandre had his cholesterol levels tested. The test showed that his cholesterol was 210 milligrams per deciliter (mg/dL). What does this equate to in the units of grams per deciliter (g/dL)?
    a) 0.021 g/dL
    b) 0.21 g/dL
    c) 2.1 g/dL
    d) 21 g/dL
    e) 210 g/dL

3. As mentioned in the passage, Daly studied the causes of heart attacks. Heart attacks are usually a result of heart disease. About 1/4 of deaths in the United States are due to heart disease. Based on this information, if there are 100 deaths, how many of them are due to heart disease?
    a) 0.25
    b) 25
    c) 40
    d) 100
    e) 140

4. After learning about Marie Maynard Daly, Kenya decided that she wanted to attain her bachelor's degree, master's degree, and doctoral degree in biochemistry. Based on the information given in the table, how many years would it take for her to attain all three degrees?
    a) 3
    b) 4
    c) 6.5
    d) 8
    e) 12

Degree	Number of Years
Bachelor's	4
Master's	1.5
PhD (doctoral)	2.5
Total	?

5. There are close to 30,000 biochemists and biophysicists in the United States. If only 600 of them are Black women, which fraction DOES NOT represent the number of Black women who are biochemists and biophysicists out of the total number of biochemists and biophysicists?
    a) 6/30,000
    b) 6/300
    c) 2/100
    d) 12/600
    e) 1/50

DO'S & DON'TS OF DIET

Unhealthy diets often include those that are high in calories, added sugar, sodium, and saturated fat. Unhealthy diets also include diets that lack sufficient fruits, vegetables, whole grains, and foods that are high in calcium and fiber. Getting too much of the unhealthy foods and not enough of the healthy foods increases the risk of many diet-related diseases. Examples of these diseases include: heart disease; diabetes; obesity; high blood pressure; stroke; osteoporosis; and cancer. Below is a list of healthy eating habits. Complete the sentence correctly by adding "Do" or "Don't". With permission from a responsible adult, use the internet to find out what some of these terms mean.

1. _____ eat more fresh fruits, vegetables, whole grains, and beans.
2. _____ drink a lot of juices that are high in sugar.
3. _____ eat foods that are high in trans-fat.
4. _____ limit saturated fat intake.
5. _____ eat a variety of foods that are high in protein.
6. _____ add a lot of salt to your food.
7. _____ skip meals and eat a lot of snacks.
8. _____ drink plenty of water.
9. _____ read and understand nutrition labels.
10. _____ eat a lot of processed foods.

WORD SEARCH PUZZLE

```
A B Z R T B E C Y U M I O P G
D I A H Q W V M C F U I S K M
H O J I U M T H X Q V G G Z S
Y C A N C E R T H G W M N J O
R H Y B X M W C A C T X U I L
N E P Z N D R F H Q E P L K O
P M G N J A K E D V I V E S R
L I A K E P M L V W D A V B E
M S A S Q I J K M T N O P Q T
Q T E Y C E S A E S I D A R S
D R D A R T E R I E S E A A E
V Y L W R Y I N C V R E A S L
X S O P Z X Y J L K H E G B O
Y A L S K D J F G H Q A Z S H
J Q P W O E I R U T Y M Z X C
```

ARTERIES – blood vessels that carry blood from the heart to other body parts
BIOCHEMISTRY – science that focuses on chemical processes in organisms
CANCER – a disease when abnormal cells grow and spread in the body
CHEMICALS – substances made of matter (any liquid, solid, or gas)
CHOLESTEROL – a type of fat in your blood that helps your organs work
DIET – the kinds of food and drinks a person consumes on a regular basis
DISEASE – a sickness that affects a person, animal, or plant
HEART – the organ that pumps blood through veins and arteries
LUNGS – organs that people and animals use to breathe in air
RESEARCH – study that is done to learn new facts and discover new things

ANNIE EASLEY
"Computer Scientist, Mathematician, & Rocket Scientist"

February 1, 2018

Dear Diary,

School was amazing today! We learned about Black scientists. My favorite, by far, was Annie Easley! Annie was born in Birmingham, Alabama in 1933. She grew up during a time when Black people were not treated fairly. However, she didn't let that discourage her. Annie's mother let her know that she could be anything that she wanted to be, as long as she worked hard. Working hard is exactly what she did. When she got older, she became a mathematician and computer scientist! How cool?!

She worked at the National Aeronautics and Space Administration (NASA). She started off at NASA as a "human computer", doing calculations by hand. As technology developed, the "human computers" were replaced by machines. So she wouldn't be out of a job, Annie became a very skilled computer programmer and learned how to write computer code. That means she wrote instructions to tell the machines what to do. Her work at NASA helped society learn more about aeronautics and aerospace.

I am happy to say that her story has inspired me! I am going to strive to be as smart, hard-working, and disciplined as Annie was.

Sincerely,
Imani

READING

The following questions are related to the passage about Annie Easley. For each question, select the best answer based on the information that you read in the passage.

1. Based on what Imani wrote about Annie Easley, Annie was all of the following EXCEPT
    a) hard-working.
    b) smart.
    c) lazy.
    d) determined.
    e) disciplined.

2. Imani's impression of Annie's mother in lines 8-9 is that she was
    a) encouraging.
    b) quiet.
    c) mean.
    d) unsupportive.
    e) boring.

3. As used in line 16, "replaced by" most likely means
    a) above.
    b) behind.
    c) next to.
    d) helping.
    e) used in place of.

4. Based on the reading, Annie Easley was all of the following EXCEPT for
    a) a mathematician.
    b) a computer scientist.
    c) a daughter.
    d) an astronaut.
    e) a NASA employee.

5. The overall tone of the reading is one of
    a) uncertainty.
    b) sadness.
    c) excitement.
    d) jealousy.
    e) anger.

WRITING

The following sentences test your ability to recognize grammatical errors. The sentences have either one error or no error at all. If the sentence has an error, circle the underlined part that contains the error. If the sentence does not contain an error, circle the choice that says "NO ERROR". After you make your selection, explain why you chose your answer.

Example: Aeronautics <u>is</u> the science of air (<u>travel aerospace</u>) is the aspect of science that <u>focuses</u> on the atmosphere and outer space. <u>NO ERROR</u>
Explanation: This is a run-on sentence because two independent clauses are joined without proper punctuation or a conjunction. To correct the error, a period or conjunction (i.e., "and") should be added after "travel".

1. Easley <u>Volunteered</u> in school tutoring programs and <u>talked to</u> students about <u>the work</u> at NASA. <u>NO ERROR</u>

   Explanation:_____
   _____
   _____

2. At NASA, <u>people</u> work hard <u>two</u> answer questions <u>about</u> outer space. <u>NO ERROR</u>

   Explanation:_____
   _____
   _____

3. Annie Easley <u>wrote</u> computer code <u>to study</u> alternative power technology that <u>was</u> used for the Centaur rocket stage. <u>NO ERROR</u>

   Explanation:_____

   _____

   _____

4. Annie <u>also</u> worked as a counselor, making sure that <u>NASA employees</u> were not discriminated against because of <u>there</u> gender, race, or age. <u>NO ERROR</u>

   Explanation:_____

   _____

   _____

5. Annie was a <u>role model</u> who inspired girls <u>and</u> students of color to pursue careers <u>in science</u>, technology, engineering, and math. <u>NO ERROR</u>

   Explanation:_____

   _____

   _____

MATH

In this section, you are presented with math problems and a set of answer choices. Read each problem carefully. Then, solve each problem to choose the best answer.

1. Annie was born in 1933 and passed away at the age of 78. In what year did she pass away?
    a) 1933
    b) 1978
    c) 2008
    d) 2011
    e) 2017

2. Annie Easley started working for NASA in 1955. She retired (stopped working) from NASA around 1989. How many years did she work at NASA?
    a) 14
    b) 34
    c) 44
    d) 55
    e) 89

3. When Annie started working at NASA, there were only a few other Black employees. If there were four Black employees and a total of 2500 employees, which of the following answers represents the fraction of Black employees out of total employees?
   a) 1/625
   b) 4/500
   c) 400/2500
   d) 1/4
   e) 2846/2500

4. Each week, Annie had to work 40 hours in six days. If she worked the same amount of time each day for those six days, which equation could be used to determine how many hours she worked each day?
   a) $40 \div 6$
   b) $40 - 6$
   c) $40 + 6$
   d) 40×6
   e) $(40 \times 6) - 6$

5. Annie developed computer code to analyze alternative power technology for the Centaur rocket stage. The original rocket stage, which is in the shape of a cylinder, is about 10 feet in diameter, d, and about 30 feet in height, h. What is the approximate volume, V, of the rocket stage? (Hint: Use the equation below. The r is radius. You can find the radius by dividing the diameter, d, by 2.)
   a) $150\ ft^3$
   b) $300\ ft^3$
   c) $150\pi\ ft^3$
   d) $300\pi\ ft^3$
   e) $750\pi\ ft^3$

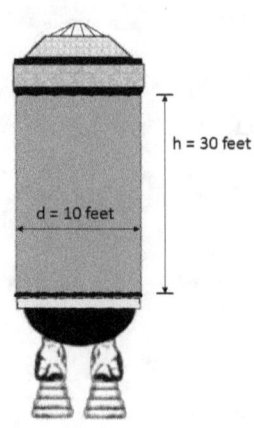

$$V = \pi \times r \times r \times h$$

WORD UNSCRAMBLE

The words below are all scrambled! Your task is to unscramble the words. They are all related to the work that Annie Easley did at NASA. If you need some help, go back to the reading passage at the beginning of this section.

r	c	p	o	t	m	u	e

i	a	n	a	a	m	t	h	e	m	t	i	c

t	s	c	i	s	e	n	t	i

c	o	s	a	l	n	i	c	u	l	a	t

a	c	e	s	m	h	i	n

a	e	g	o	m	m	p	r	r	r

n	y	t	g	o	l	o	e	c	h

c	e	r	o	s	e	a	p	a

COMPUTER CODING

A computer program is a set of clear instructions that tells the computer exactly what to do. Write a program that tells the computer how to get through this maze. Your instructions should tell the computer which direction (right, left, up, or down) to move and how far. The first 4 commands have been done for you. Give it a try!

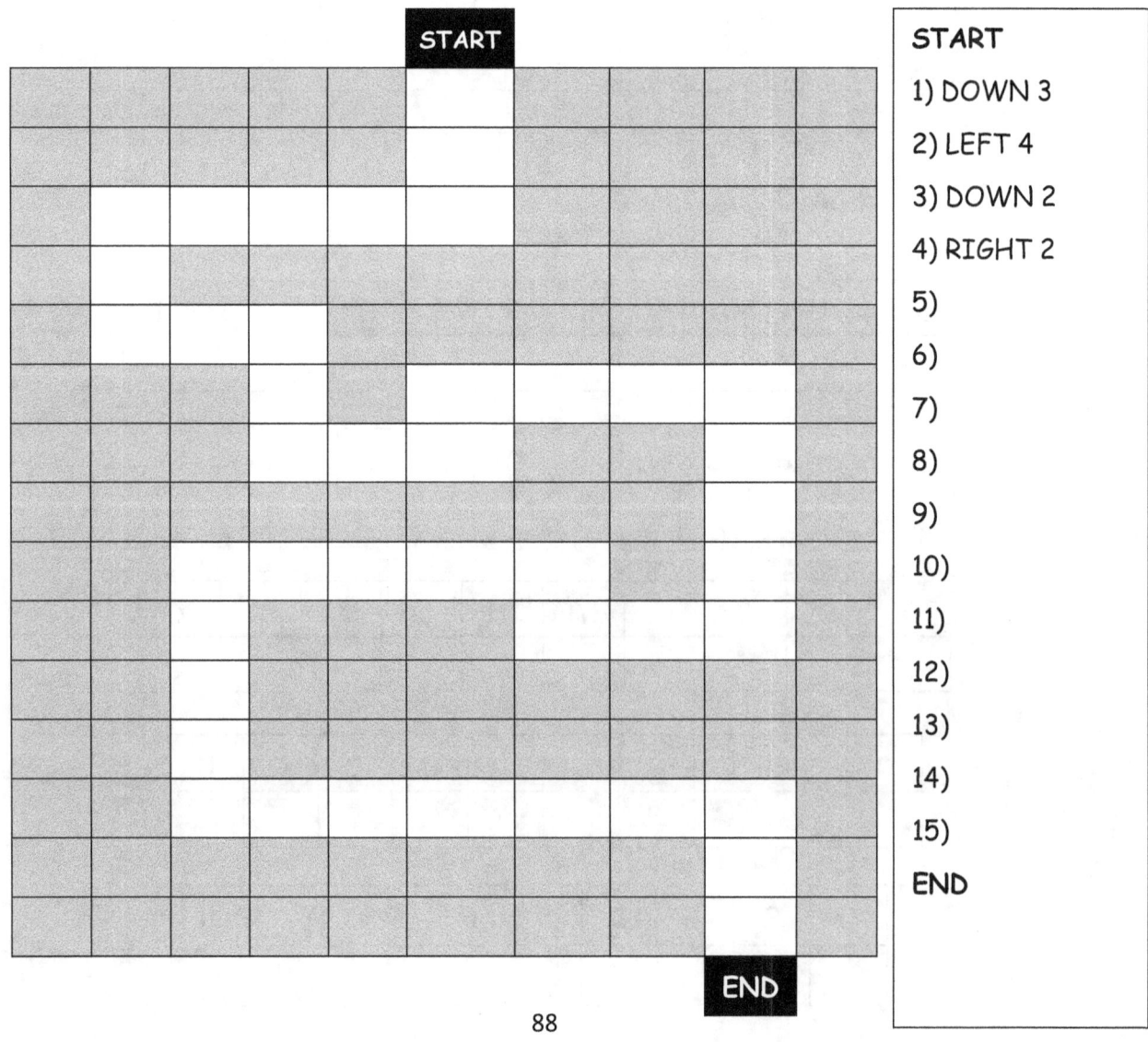

START
1) DOWN 3
2) LEFT 4
3) DOWN 2
4) RIGHT 2
5)
6)
7)
8)
9)
10)
11)
12)
13)
14)
15)
END

PATRICIA BATH

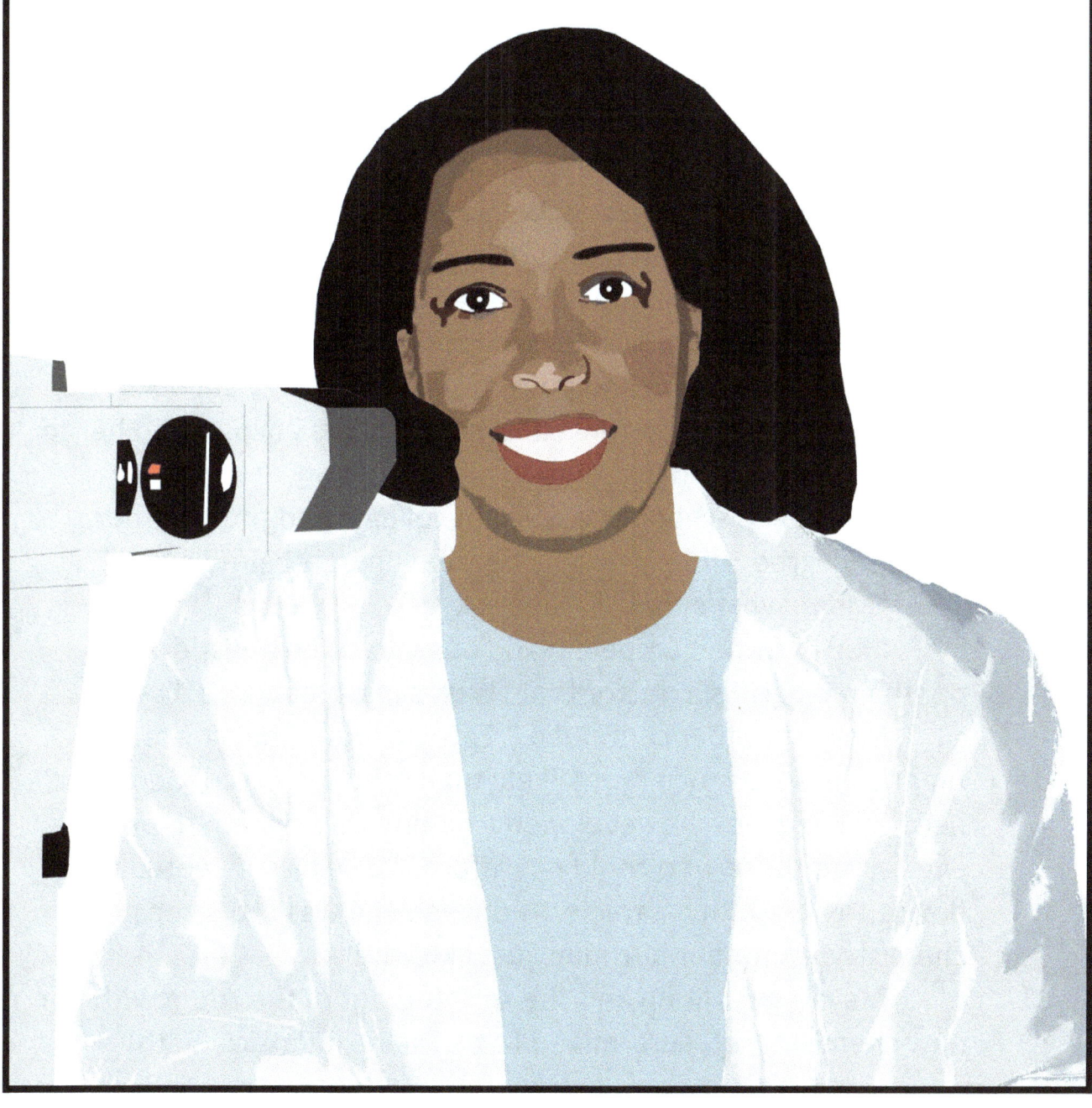

PATRICIA BATH
"Inventor, Doctor, & Educator"

"Mommy!!! Daddy!!!" Maya exclaimed when she opened her birthday gift. "You remembered! I said that I wanted a chemistry set for my birthday and you remembered!"

"Yes, we did!" Maya's mother responded. "But, before you use it, you have to let me tell you a story about a little girl who grew up to do wonderful things."

Thinking that she would be bored by her mother's story, Maya grudgingly responded, "ookkaayy!"

"The little girl's name is Patricia Bath. Patricia grew up with her mother, father, and siblings in Harlem, New York. Though she faced issues like racism and poverty, she had a very supportive community. Both her parents and her teachers encouraged her to be great. And she did just that!"

"After high school, she went to college, and then got her medical degree, and eventually became an ophthalmologist."

"Mom, what's that?" Maya asked.

Maya's father jumped in and answered the question. "An ophthalmologist is a doctor that studies and treats eye diseases."

Maya's mother continued. "Patricia found that African-Americans were much more likely than other groups of people to become blind. So, she developed a community system to provide eye care to those who could not afford it. She also invented a device to help with cataracts. And when she was little, she got a chemistry set for her birthday, just like you!"

Maya's eyes lit up and she sprinted out of the room with her new chemistry set, determined to be the next Patricia Bath!

READING

The following questions are related to the passage about Patricia Bath. For each question, select the best answer based on the information that you read in the passage.

1. In line 8 of the story, the word "grudgingly" is used. Which of the words below could NOT be used to replace "grudgingly"?
    a) unwillingly
    b) hesitantly
    c) happily
    d) reluctantly
    e) unenthusiastically

2. Which answer best describes what happens in the passage?
    a) Maya plays with her chemistry set.
    b) Maya's parents tell her a story about Patricia Bath.
    c) Patricia Bath talks to Maya about college.
    d) Maya's father tells her what an ophthalmologist is.
    e) Maya has a birthday party.

3. As used in line 25, "sprinted" means
    a) sat down.
    b) cried.
    c) called someone on the phone.
    d) ran.
    e) looked.

4. The sentence "Maya's eyes...the next Patricia Bath!" (lines 25-26), suggests that Maya was
    a) sad.
    b) sleepy.
    c) excited.
    d) cold.
    e) funny.

5. The purpose of Maya's parents telling her the story about Patricia Bath was most likely to
    a) teach her about chemistry.
    b) discourage Maya from being a medical doctor.
    c) make fun of Patricia Bath.
    d) watch Maya run out of the room.
    e) encourage Maya to be great like Patricia Bath.

WRITING

The following sentences test your ability to recognize grammatical errors. The sentences have either one error or no error at all. If the sentence has an error, circle the underlined part that contains the error. If the sentence does not contain an error, circle the choice that says "NO ERROR". After you make your selection, explain why you chose your answer.

Example: A <u>cataract is a</u> clouding <u>of the</u> lens in the ⟨<u>eye. which</u>⟩ leads to blurred vision. <u>NO ERROR</u>

Explanation: The period should be deleted. A period should be used at the end, not in the middle, of a complete statement.

---

1. Patricia Bath <u>are</u> the first African-American <u>female doctor</u> to patent <u>a</u> medical device. <u>NO ERROR</u>

    Explanation: _____

    _____

    _____

2. Patricia <u>Bath's</u> daughter also <u>grew</u> up <u>2</u> be a medical doctor. <u>NO ERROR</u>

    Explanation: _____

    _____

    _____

3. <u>An</u> ophthalmologist <u>is</u> a <u>type of</u> medical doctor. <u>NO ERROR</u>

   Explanation:_____
   _____
   _____

4. Many Black families <u>moved</u> from cities <u>in</u> the South to Harlem, New York <u>between</u> the 1910s and 1930s. <u>NO ERROR</u>

   Explanation:_____
   _____
   _____

5. Like Patricia Bath, you should use <u>you're</u> skills <u>and</u> talents to help <u>your</u> community. <u>NO ERROR</u>

   Explanation:_____
   _____
   _____

MATH

In this section, you are presented with math problems and a set of answer choices. Read each problem carefully. Then, solve each problem to choose the best answer.

1. Patricia Bath was born in 1942. About how old was she when she graduated from medical school in 1968?
    a) 19 years old
    b) 26 years old
    c) 36 years old
    d) 42 years old
    e) 68 years old

2. In order to become an ophthalmologist, one typically has to attend 4 years of undergraduate college for their bachelor's degree, 4 years of medical school for their medical degree, and 3 years of training in ophthalmology. How many total years does it take someone to become an ophthalmologist?
    a) 3
    b) 4
    c) 7
    d) 11
    e) 14

3. If there are close to 900,000 medical doctors in the U.S. and nearly 1/5 of them are ophthalmologists, about how many medical doctors are ophthalmologists?
    a) 150,000
    b) 180,000
    c) 200,000
    d) 250,000
    e) 300,000

4. Throughout the world, there are about 36 million people who are blind. If there are six times as many people who have low vision, how many total people are either blind or have low vision?
    a) 42 million
    b) 136 million
    c) 236 million
    d) 246 million
    e) 252 million

5. A person's field of view can be defined by how much they can see at a given time. The figure below shows a person's horizontal field of view. If the total field of view is 220° and the black section is 114°, what is the value of x?
    a) 35°
    b) 53°
    c) 106°
    d) 114°
    e) 220°

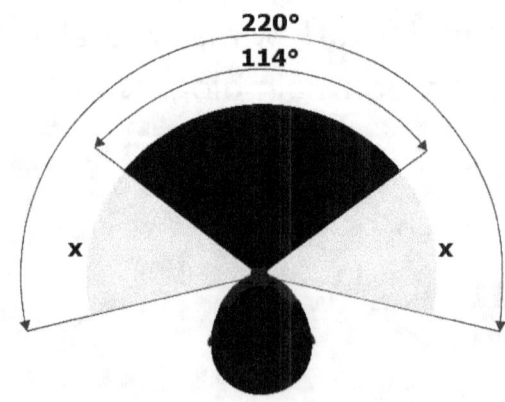

EYE HEALTH

There are many eye conditions. Some of the conditions are hereditary (passed down in your family) and some of the conditions are acquired over time. Fill in the table below to learn more about different eye conditions. You may need to use the internet or an encyclopedia for help. The first one is done for you as an example.

What is the eye condition?	How is the condition caused?	How can you prevent the condition?	If you already have the eye condition, what are ways to treat it?
Glaucoma - a condition that causes damage to the optic nerve in your eye	a buildup of pressure inside the eye	− Exercise regularly − Lower your insulin levels	− Take eye drops or pills to reduce pressure in the eye − Get laser treatment − Have surgery

INVENTOR

The medical device that Patricia Bath invented is called the Laserphaco Probe. This device "created a less painful and more precise treatment of cataracts." Using the device, she was able to restore the sight of people who were blind. Now it is your turn to be creative and invent a device that can help cure an illness! With the permission of a responsible adult, look up medical devices on the internet to gain inspiration from past inventions. Draw your invention below and write a few sentences to explain what it is and how it works.

MAE C. JEMISON
"Mother to Daughter: Blast Off!"

"Mommy! Guess who came in to talk to my class for career day?" the little girl asked with great excitement. "An astronaut!!" She spat out the answer before her mother even had a chance to guess. "But...," the little girl's feeling of excitement quickly changed to one of great sadness.

"But what?" the little girl's mother asked.

"Black girls can't be astronauts. Black people don't do that kind of stuff."

"Nonsense!" the little girl's mother exclaimed. "There are many Black astronauts, both past and present. Have you ever heard of Mae C. Jemison?"

"No. Who is that?" the little girl asked with a doubtful inquisitiveness.

"Well, sit down and let me tell you about her. Mae C. Jemison grew up in Chicago, Illinois. Just like you, she had a strong interest in math and science. So, when she went to college, she decided to get a degree in chemical engineering and a doctorate degree in medicine. But that wasn't all she studied while she was in college. She also received a degree in African-American Studies. She recognized that she had to learn about her history and culture in order to figure out how she could help her family, her friends, and her community.

"After she got her degrees, she became a general practitioner. That's a type of medical doctor. She even spent time in Africa, helping to improve the health care system and doing research to find cures to diseases."

Her mother continued. "And in 1992...she did it!"

"Did what, mommy???" The little girl was now on the edge of her seat, eager for her mother to continue the story.

"She, along with her teammates, blasted off on the Space Shuttle *Endeavor*. This trip into outer space made her the first African-American woman astronaut! She was the science mission specialist on the team. She was on-board to work on a bone cell research experiment. After her experience as an astronaut, she became a college professor and she founded her own technology company."

"Wow!" the little girl exclaimed. "That sounds like a lot of work. Does she ever have time to have fun?!"

"Oh, of course! Even though Mae is best known for being an astronaut, she is very well-rounded. She enjoys her work, but when she is not working, Mae has lots of hobbies to keep her busy. She enjoys dancing, exercising, reading, collecting African art, traveling, and much more! She even speaks multiple languages including English, Russian, Japanese, and Swahili! Most importantly, she has dedicated her life to being a positive role model!"

The little girl jumped out of the chair and ran out of the room. "Where are you going?" the mother yelled.

"To become an astronaut!!!" the little girl exclaimed.

READING

The following questions are related to the passage about Mae C. Jemison. For each question, select the best answer based on the information that you read in the passage.

1. The most likely reason for the little girl's feeling changing from "excitement" to "sadness" in lines 1-5 is that
    a) she forgot what happened during career day.
    b) her mother said something to make her sad.
    c) she didn't believe that she could be an astronaut.
    d) she didn't give her mother a chance to guess.
    e) her mother didn't believe her.

2. In lines 16-17, the little girl asked a question with a doubtful inquisitiveness. Based on context clues, "doubtful inquisitiveness" suggests that the little girl was
    a) unconvinced but curious.
    b) uninterested.
    c) acting silly.
    d) irritated and confused.
    e) certain.

3. The word "eager", as used in line 36, means
    a) confused.
    b) anxious.
    c) mad.
    d) happy.
    e) bored.

4. The purpose of the sentence "She was on-board to work on a bone cell research experiment" (lines 41-42), is most likely to
    a) confuse the little girl.
    b) bring up a random fact that has nothing to do with the story.
    c) be funny.
    d) rephrase something that the mother said earlier.
    e) explain what Jemison did as a science mission specialist.

5. Based on the passage, which of the following is NOT mentioned as an interest of Mae C. Jemison?
    a) traveling
    b) hunting
    c) exercising
    d) reading
    e) collecting art

WRITING

The following sentences test your ability to recognize grammatical errors. The sentences have either one error or no error at all. If the sentence has an error, circle the underlined part that contains the error. If the sentence does not contain an error, circle the choice that says "NO ERROR". After you make your selection, explain why you chose your answer.

Example: Mae C. <u>Jemison, who</u> was always interested in math <u>and</u> science, became <u>(a)</u> astronaut. <u>NO ERROR</u>

Explanation: The error is "a". As a rule, "a" is used before words that begin with a consonant and "an" is used before words that begin with a vowel. Since "astronaut" starts with a vowel, "an" should be used.

1. Mae C. Jemison <u>growed</u> up in <u>Chicago, Illinois</u> with her mother, father, <u>and siblings</u>. <u>NO ERROR</u>

   Explanation:_____
   _____
   _____

2. In 1992, the space shuttle "Voyager" <u>will blast</u> into space <u>and</u> orbited the <u>earth</u>. <u>NO ERROR</u>

   Explanation:_____
   _____
   _____

3. A role model <u>are</u> a person <u>whose</u> behavior in a certain role <u>is imitated</u> by other people. <u>NO ERROR</u>

   Explanation: _____

   _____

   _____

4. The members <u>of</u> the astronaut crew <u>include</u> the pilot or commander <u>and</u> mission specialists. <u>NO ERROR</u>

   Explanation: _____

   _____

   _____

5. Mae Jemison <u>worked</u> as a doctor <u>in various</u> African countries, <u>including</u> Liberia and Sierra Leone. <u>NO ERROR</u>

   Explanation: _____

   _____

   _____

MATH

In this section, you are presented with math problems and a set of answer choices. Read each problem carefully. Then, solve each problem to choose the best answer.

1. Mae Jemison was only 16 years old when she started college in 1973. How old was she when she graduated in 1977?
    a) 17 years old
    b) 18 years old
    c) 19 years old
    d) 20 years old
    e) 21 years old

2. The Super-Duper Astronaut Team took three trips to space. Trip A lasted 10.25 days, Trip B lasted 11.5 days, and Trip C lasted 12 days. How many total days did all three trips take, rounded to the nearest tenth?
    a) 31.8 days
    b) 33.25 days
    c) 33.7 days
    d) 33.75 days
    e) 33.8 days

3. The astronauts on the Super-Duper Astronaut Team had to take 16 classes for training. They had to complete each class before starting the next one. If each class lasted for 40 days, how many days did it take for them to finish all of their classes?
    a) 164
    b) 365
    c) 600
    d) 640
    e) 1640

4. Mae C. Jemison was in space for 7 days and 22 hours. How many total hours was she in space?
    a) 7 hours
    b) 22 hours
    c) 24 hours
    d) 154 hours
    e) 190 hours

5. All of the planets in the universe are shaped like a sphere. If the sphere below has a radius, r, of 3 meters, what is the volume, V, of the sphere?
    a) 3π meters^3
    b) 9π meters^3
    c) 27π meters^3
    d) 36π meters^3
    e) 108π meters^3

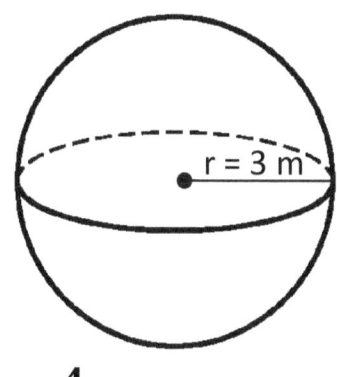

$$V = \frac{4}{3}\pi \times r \times r \times r$$

BLAST OFF INTO SPACE!

Use your problem-solving skills to solve this maze. Start at the rocket and find a clear path to the planet. Blast off!

ANCIENT ASTROLOGY

The Dogon are a group of people who live in Mali, a country in West Africa. Like many groups from Africa, the Dogon are in tune with the universe. For thousands of years, the Dogon have interpreted symbols and preserved vast amounts of secret astronomical knowledge. This knowledge teaches them a lot about life here on earth. By decoding the sentence below, you will learn one of the many exciting facts about the Dogon.

IN 1862, AN AMERICAN ASTRONOMER DISCOVERED SIRIUS B, A STAR THAT THE DOGON PEOPLE DISCOVERED MANY YEARS EARLIER WITHOUT USING A TELESCOPE.

@	&	¢	đ	≡	‡	?	#	!	⌐	ℏ	‖	Σ
A	B	C	D	E	F	G	H	I	J	K	L	M

∩	○	℘	Ω	㆐	$	†	υ	√	♁	×	λ	≠
N	O	P	Q	R	S	T	U	V	W	X	Y	Z

www.ingramcontent.com/pod-product-compliance
Lightning Source LLC
Chambersburg PA
CBHW081359290426
44110CB00018B/2429